THE OFFICIAL
SIDEKICK
HANDBOOK

THE OFFICIAL
SIDEKICK
HANDBOOK

HOW TO UNLEASH YOUR
INNER SECOND BANANA AND
FIND TRUE HAPPINESS

TOO SLIM & TEXAS BIX BENDER

ILLUSTRATIONS BY JAMES HOUGH

GIBBS SMITH
TO ENRICH AND INSPIRE HUMANKIND

First Edition
15 14 13 12 11   5 4 3 2 1

Text © 2011 Too Slim and Texas Bix Bender
Illustrations © 2011 James Hough
Page 38, 71, 100 photos by Gabi Rona / mptvimages.com
Page 47, 58 photos © 2000 Glenn Weiner / mptvimages.com
Page 54 photo by Bud Gray / mptvimages.com
Page 115 photo courtesy of Riders In The Sky

Published by
Gibbs Smith
P.O. Box 667
Layton, Utah 84041

1.800.835.4993 orders
www.gibbs-smith.com

Designed by Michel Vrána
Printed and bound in the U.S.A.

Gibbs Smith books are printed on either recycled, 100% post-consumer
waste, FSC-certified papers or on paper produced from sustainable PEFC-
certified forest/controlled wood source. Learn more at www.pefc.org.

Library of Congress Cataloging-in-Publication Data

LaBour, Fred.
   The official sidekick handbook : how to unleash your inner second banana and find true happiness / Too Slim, Texas
Bix Bender ; illustrations by James Hough. — 1st ed.
      p. cm.
   ISBN 978-1-4236-1920-8
   1. American wit and humor. 2. Conduct of life—Humor.
3. Heroes—Humor. I. Bender, Texas Bix, 1949- II. Title.
   PN6165.L33 2011
   818'.5402—dc22
                                        2010042660

CONTENTS

ACKNOWLEDGMENTS

We would like to acknowledge the invaluable ideas of Gibbs Smith, Madge Baird, the capable crew in Laytonland, and the "Picasso of the Prairie," James Hough. And most especially the tireless efforts of our patient, intrepid editor (and future stand-up comedy star) Lisa Anderson.

Too Slim would like to acknowledge the generous grant from the LaBour Foundation for Non-Institutional Living, which funded his research and writing. Texas Bix would like to know what happened to HIS grant.

Too Slim also thanks Ranger Doug, Woody Paul, and Joey the CPK for providing him the opportunity to be "the only western sidekick currently making a living."

THE OFFICIAL
SIDEKICK
HANDBOOK

WHY A SIDEKICK?

REASONS AND RATIONALES

LOOK AT ALL THOSE OTHER BOOKS ON THE SELF- help shelf. What do they all have in common? A relentless striving to be Number One, that's what. A crazy desire for Top o' the Heap-dom. An absurd need to sacrifice time, energy, psychic and emotional resources, and your very identity in mad pursuit of winning, whatever "winning" means.

Must you be the fastest rat in the race? Are you condemned to endless grasping for fleeting glory in order to find fulfill-ment? Does your hair have to be THAT perfect? Do you have to keep late hours and never get enough sleep because somebody else might get "ahead" of you, whatever "ahead" means? Is your only future the shouldering of miserable re-sponsibilities and worrying about that extra fifteen pounds?

No, there is another way. And this book will show it to you.

WHY BE A SIDEKICK?
REASONS AND RATIONALES

1 Sidekicks are always forgiven. Go ahead, screw it up. You don't have to be perfect. Use the Power of Low Expectations!

2 Avoid the heavy lifting while enjoying co-billing.

3 Eat what you want! Loosen your belt and take a nap. Who cares? You're just a sidekick!

The Sidekick Solution, my weary friend, to the rescue.

We are convinced that deep inside most of us is an inner sidekick, a self happy to settle for less, lower those sights, and trade the constant struggle for "success," whatever "success" means, for a comfortable, fulfilling, stress-free life as Second Banana. Plus, you can eat what you want.

We're not talking about slacking here, or extolling the virtues of laziness. We're talking about "The Art of Under-Achieving," "The Seven Habits of the Highly Mediocre," "The Power of Positive . . . ly Letting Someone Else Hog the Spotlight While You Do Just Fine, Thank You Very Much." Here, hungry pilgrim, is "Chicken Soup for the Sidekick."

Do you have what it takes to be a Sidekick? Yes, you do, and these pages will show you how.

ARE YOU SIDEKICK MATERIAL?

If you want to be Numero Uno, the Big Cheese, the Head Honcho, Mr. Big Shot, this book isn't for you. This book is for everybody else.

How can you tell if you're "everybody else?" Simple. Stand naked in front of a full-length mirror. Yeow! Sorry. Stand casually clothed in front of a full-length mirror. Now, which character on the next page do you resemble?

HERO

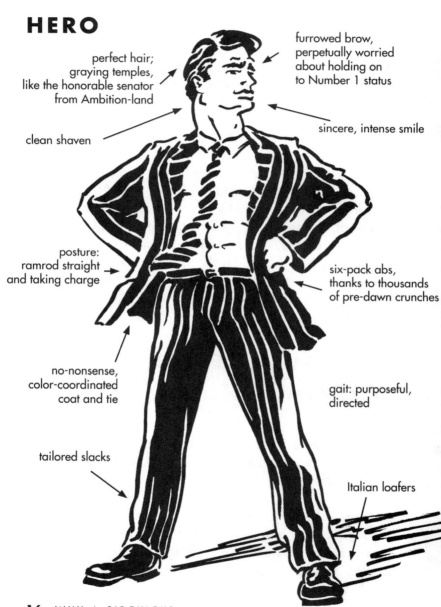

perfect hair; graying temples, like the honorable senator from Ambition-land

furrowed brow, perpetually worried about holding on to Number 1 status

clean shaven

sincere, intense smile

posture: ramrod straight and taking charge

six-pack abs, thanks to thousands of pre-dawn crunches

no-nonsense, color-coordinated coat and tie

gait: purposeful, directed

tailored slacks

Italian loafers

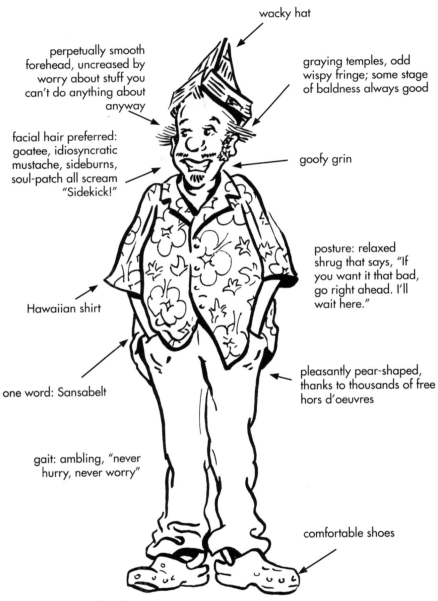

wacky hat

perpetually smooth forehead, uncreased by worry about stuff you can't do anything about anyway

graying temples, odd wispy fringe; some stage of baldness always good

facial hair preferred: goatee, idiosyncratic mustache, sideburns, soul-patch all scream "Sidekick!"

goofy grin

posture: relaxed shrug that says, "If you want it that bad, go right ahead. I'll wait here."

Hawaiian shirt

one word: Sansabelt

pleasantly pear-shaped, thanks to thousands of free hors d'oeuvres

gait: ambling, "never hurry, never worry"

comfortable shoes

SIDEKICK

So, you definitely lean in the sidekick direction but you're still unsure if you have genuine sidekick blood in your veins. You're not alone.

Academics have debated for decades whether sidekicks are born or made, with the discussion turning ugly at the "2010 UC-Santa Cruz Symposium on Nature vs. Nurture in Sidekick Identification and Subsequent Personality Development." During the presentation of Dr. B. Baxter Bazzle's paper entitled "That Doggone DNA Don't Lie," incensed colleagues stood on chairs, hooted and made monkey sounds until a shaken Bazzle left the podium. (He retired from public speaking that night.)

The fact is that the Human Genome Project has failed, at this writing, to discern a gene indisputably linked to sidekick traits. Says one researcher: "We have found a gene for letting another warrior run in front and take a spear in the chest; we have found a gene for an amused grin and shrug; we have even found a gene for a predilection for odd cranial coverings, or, as you might say, hats. But a gene which is directly responsible for the sensible humility of a true sidekick eludes us. It may not exist."

In short, it's up to you. Take responsibility for your own sidekick life, and genetic heritage or not, join the happy evolutionary trend to successfully standing just outside the spotlight.

"A journey of a thousand miles begins with a single tank of gas."

—Wu Hu Hunan,
sidekick to Mao Zedong

WHY WE SAY "SIDEKICK"

Why not "useful pal?" Or "banana of the lower tier?" Or "guy with wacky hat who keeps the plot interesting with humorous asides and japes?"

Scholars from a prestigious midwestern land grant university, with abundant time on their hands, have determined that the term "sidekick" has, perhaps, descended from the Middle English *kiken*, meaning "wallet" or "pocket," and first appeared in 1530. As years rolled by, "kiken" became "kick."

Mid-nineteenth century pickpockets, a reliable source of colorful language, referred to the front side pockets of a man's trousers—traditionally the most difficult to pick—as, you guessed it, the "side kicks." Mid-nineteenth-century pickpockets often worked in tandem. A partner providing diversion—a bump, an odd noise, an inquiry for directions to the premier local grog shop—could be used to flummox the victim and open the way for a successful "side kick" pick. Say THAT six times real fast.

Such a partner would have to be trustworthy, capable, and close enough to the primary perpetrator to support the enterprise, split the spoils, and not gum up the works by hogging the spotlight and demanding star treatment . . . all indicators of a true SIDEKICK.

SIDEKICK PERSONALITY QUIZ

Do you have what it takes to be a sidekick? Take this personality quiz and find out if a rewarding life as a Second Banana can be yours!

❶ YOU'RE ENJOYING A SUNDAY DRIVE IN THE COUNTRY. BANG! A BLOWOUT! YOU COME TO A STOP WITH A FLAT TIRE. YOU . . .

A. Change the tire.

B. Order someone else to change the tire.

C. Say you've just about had it with all of this BS, pull out a revolver, and shoot wildly in all directions.

D. Start taking the tools out of the trunk, drop the jack humorously on your toe, and hop around on one foot until someone says, "Hey, better let me handle this."

❷ YOU'RE IN CHARGE OF A SYSTEMS MANAGEMENT DEPARTMENT WHEN WORD COMES DOWN THAT IT'S TIME TO DOWNSIZE. YOU . . .

A. Call a meeting with employees where you clearly articulate options, empathetically listen to concerns, and make a tough situation tolerable with your fairness and honesty.

B. Suddenly remember you're needed in Miami for two weeks and order someone to handle it while you're away.

C. Say you've just about had it with all of this BS, pull out a revolver, and shoot wildly in all directions.

D. Call a meeting, pass out cream pies all around, and start a food fight.

❸ **YOUR FIFTEEN-YEAR-OLD ANNOUNCES THAT "SCHOOL IS FOR LOSERS" AND SHE'S LEAVING HOME TO PURSUE HER DREAM OF BECOMING A POLE DANCER ON THE BLUEGRASS MUSIC CIRCUIT. YOU . . .**

MINI PEARL OF WISDOM

We overheard Minnie Pearl, the brilliant comedienne, beloved humanitarian and sidekick to Roy Acuff, "The King of Country Music," being interviewed at the next table. The reporter asked her the secret of her show business longevity, and how she viewed the current crop of "one-hit wonders."

"I never wanted to be on the top of the hill," she said. "Somebody's always tryin' to knock you off. It's better to be in the middle. You last longer. You can take the smaller fairs, the smaller shows, and you get more work."

A. Consult with trusted advisors, schedule counseling, and say, "It doesn't matter where this journey leads, Honey. I'll be with you."

B. Answer with, "That's nice, dear. Talk to your Mom," and go back to watching full-contact golf on TV.

C. Say you've just about had it with all of this BS, pull out a revolver, and shoot wildly in all directions.

D. Retrieve Uncle Bub's banjo from the attic, wink and hop around while picking out "Polly Wolly Doodle."

④ YOUR BOSS CALLS YOU INTO HER OFFICE AND SAYS SHE'S HAD HER EYE ON YOU, THINKS YOU'RE CAPABLE OF GREATER THINGS, AND SHE'S GIVING YOU A TON OF NEW RESPONSIBILITIES, WHICH WILL REQUIRE YOU TO WORK UNTIL 10 EVERY NIGHT AND SOME WEEKENDS. YOU . . .

A. Embrace the opportunity and say things like "I'm your man" and "Sleep is over-rated."

B. Exclaim, "Fabulous news!" And later quietly arrange for Ferguson in accounting to cover any extra work.

C. Say you've just about had it with all of this BS, pull out a revolver, and shoot wildly in all directions.

D. Say "Great idea!," compliment her hair, reach to shake hands, knocking photos off her desk, and execute a pratfall into the file cabinet. Suggest that someone of HER capabilities should really be the one with new responsibilities, but you'll always be there to advise and consult, and why not discuss it over lunch as soon as you change into your Hawaiian shirt.

⑤ THE EVIL VILLAIN SLOCUM HAS TIED MISS MARM, THE TOWN'S LOVELY SELF-ACTUALIZED SCHOOL TEACHER, TO THE RAILROAD TRACKS. SOON NOTHING WILL STAND BETWEEN HIM AND OWNING THE WHOLE VALLEY. YOU . . .

POEM I SING THE SECOND BANANA

(Heretofore unknown Walt Whitman poem, apparently rejected in 1857 by *New York Post-Tribune* editors as ". . . dim, annoying drivel, perhaps better suited to a future, less rigorous, century.")

I sing the Second Banana
Who stands one rung below
Chasing not the fleeting glory
Where the grasping Heroes go.
A Fruit of equal succulence
To any in the bunch
Content to ripen in the Sun
And take a three-hour Lunch.
Let Heroes mighty sweat and strain
To fight and win, grim spoils to gain
While the wise Penultimate Banana,
Knows the Sidekick's sweet Nirvana.

A. Ride a wondrous white horse to the rescue, complete an astounding gymnastic tumble, disarm Slocum and knock him on his butt with one mighty punch, and pull Miss Marm from harm's way with a tenth of a second to spare.

B. Notice some kind of fracas over there past the hill, and head into town to alert Homeland Security that there might be a problem.

C. Say you've just about had it with all of this BS, pull out a revolver, and shoot wildly in all directions.

PATRICK STAR

Patrick Star, dumb as the rock he lives under, nevertheless has the sidekick smarts to provide endless plot lines for *SpongeBob SquarePants*.

A classic heroic role is to save the sidekick from himself, and that's what the good-hearted SpongeBob is called upon to do, by removing the sausage lei from Patrick's neck so the sea lion will stop trying to eat him. By explaining that "Mayonnaise is not an instrument." By suggesting that Patrick might aim a little lower in life than his stated goal of "defeating the giant monkey-men and saving the ninth dimension."

A salute to you, Patrick! You've kicked open the revolving door to the sidekick life, been mangled and cut in two in the process, and proved that there's a place in the Sidekick Pantheon for the truly clueless.

D. Stay oblivious to Miss Marm's peril because you've screwed up and locked yourself in a shack full of dynamite which is about to blow, requiring the hero to make still another rescue before he even has time for Miss Marm's grateful kiss.

❺ YOU HAVE A DEADLINE TO WRITE A BOOK ABOUT SIDEKICKS. YOU . . .

A. Write the book.

B. Go to the beach and suggest your co-author write the book while you're away.

C. Say you've just about had it with all of this BS, pull out a revolver, and shoot wildly in all directions.

D. Take your editor to lunch. Order cream pies all around and start a food fight.

IF YOU ANSWERED THESE QUESTIONS . . .

A. Sorry, you're a Hero.

B. Sorry, you're a Delegator.

C. Sorry, and, whatever you do, don't forget your meds!

D. Congratulations! You have sidekick blood in your veins! Now go out and find a hero!

GABBY HAYES

We had a late breakfast with Dale Evans at an IHOP in Victorville, California, one day a decade or two ago, and when the conversation turned to sidekicks, she said, "Everybody loved Gabby." True enough. She loved Gabby; she said so. You could tell by the pleasant affection in Roy Rogers' eyes during scenes with his irascible sidekick that he loved Gabby, and most assuredly us kids in the theater audience loved Gabby. In fact, we could hardly wait for the singing and yodeling to stop so Gabby could get a little more screen time with a "Dadburn it, Roy," or a "Yer durn tootin'!" or even a "durn persnickety female."

George "Gabby" Hayes retired from vaudeville to Long Island and then lost everything in the stock market debacle of 1929. He moved to Los Angeles at the urging of his wife, Olive, learned to ride a horse, and appeared in hundreds of westerns as sidekick to Hopalong Cassidy, John Wayne, Roy Rogers, and Wild Bill Elliot. Gabby, by all accounts an articulate and intelligent actor, favored fine wine and tweed in real life. Roy told us stories of Gabby pulling onto the studio lot in an elegant automobile and disembarking near the makeup trailer, where he would shed his tailored suit, don his battered hat and shapeless britches, and carefully take out his false teeth and place them in a waiting water glass, transforming into every child's best friend.

For your acting chops, your double takes, your interior sweetness, and your contribution to our childhood imaginations, we salute you, Gabby Hayes. "Yer durn tootin'," that's why.

TEST YOUR SIDEKICK I.Q.

Hey, Sidekicks-in-Training! Get out your crayons and play "Match the Sidekick with the Hero!" For extra fun, imagine each hero with a random sidekick and act out scenes with your friends. Start with Capt. Kirk and Tonto, Mick Jagger and Bullwinkle, and Batman and Boo Boo.

HERO	SIDEKICK
Don Quixote	Andy Richter
Batman	Boswell
Prince Hal	Festus
Mr. Peabody	Sancho Panza
Rocket J. Squirrel	Gabby Hayes
Conan O'Brien	Ed McMahon
Dr. Johnson	Tonto
Mick Jagger	Kramer
Moses	Robin
Sherlock Holmes	Enkidu
Capt. Kirk	Bullwinkle
Roy Rogers	Sherman
The Green Hornet	Falstaff
Gilgamesh	Boo Boo Bear
Bush 41	Paul Shaffer
The Lone Ranger	Mr. Spock
Johnny Carson	Barney Rubble
Marshall Dillon	Aaron
Yogi Bear	Keith Richards
Fred Flintstone	Dr. Watson
Jerry Seinfeld	Kato
David Letterman	Dan Quayle

"I'll be back here, way back here, holding the horses!"

—Major Barnaby Buhl,
surviving sidekick of Gen. Geo. A. Custer

CHAPTER ONE

YOU CAN'T BE A

SIDEKICK

BY YOURSELF

TIPS ON FINDING A HERO

OKAY, YOU'RE JUST OUT OF GRAD SCHOOL. Employment opportunities are limited. The sweet sidekick life is looking better and better. What's the next step? Find a hero!

One type of hero is easy to find: the Established Hero. You can find the Established Heroes behind the wheels of their shiny cars, going to countless important meetings, holding court at the best tables in the steakhouse, multitasking on their treadmills, and looking fabulous.

The problems here are access (that pesky entourage) and timing. These heroes very likely have already accumulated a sidekick or two. Indeed, they may attribute some of their success to a sidekick. If you can gain access, you can give it a shot, but you'll have to eventually deal with the negative connotations of "worming," as in "worming your way in." This can be tricky and it's derailed many a Sidekick Express.

But there's another way and another kind of hero: the Future Hero. Yes, hitch your sidekick wagon to a star. An up-and-coming star.

No access problem with a Future Hero, because nobody cares about him so there is no annoying entourage. Yet. You might gain access and win the Future Hero's confidence by doing something as simple and inexpensive as buying the table a pitcher of beer.

And there's no sidekick already in position to gum things up. The Future Hero is used to doing things on his own. But it's a lonely life, crawling your way to the top, and you will help

SIDEKICKS
AND GENDER

One easy way to attach yourself to a hero, assuming they're
of the opposite gender, or at least you're in the right state, is
to marry him or her (see Sidekicks and Marriage, page 101).

This brings up the larger issue of Sidekicks and Gender. Can
a man be a sidekick to a woman? Yes. Can a woman be a
sidekick to a man? Yes. Can a man be a sidekick to a man?
Yes. Can a woman be a sidekick to a woman? Yes.

We hope this answers all questions of Sidekicks and Gender.

him realize, by golly, he needs a sidekick, an indispensable pal to make him laugh and share the ups and downs of his trek to success.

How, then, to identify a Future Hero? It may be helpful to contrast the Future Hero with the Future Slacker, that bum at the end of the bar talking Rilke.

Look for good hair, punctuality, ambition, and focus. You want a self-starting dynamo who hums "New York, New York" and "My Way" to himself in the restroom. He's planning to wake up one morning and find he's on "top of the heap," and that future "king of the hill" is going to need a wacky companion.

(It's always helpful, though not necessary, for the Future Hero to be in line to inherit tons of money. This can lead to what we call the Sidekick Slam Dunkaroo.)

Next up: the crucial step of INGRATIATION.

INGRATIATION: CEMENTING SIDEKICK STATUS

Gaining favor with a prospective hero can be a tricky maneuver. A true hero, although susceptible to flattery and some degree of blatant buttering up, is often intelligent enough to realize he's the target of someone's ambitious ploy (see The Slime Factor).

He classifies the flatterer as an underling—perhaps useful, but not worthy of admittance to the inner circle, that hallowed ground where sidekicks tread.

Here's where commonality can help. "Hey, I'm from Peewaukee too!" Or "Nice hat! Are the Dawgs gonna get that defense together this year?" Or "Nothing like good old Dee-troit iron, is what I always say," can start the conversation.

Then see if you can illustrate a skill, some action that elevates you from nameless backslapper to beneficial buddy. "No church key? Here, I'll open it with my eyelid." Or "Watch it, you'll blow up the battery. Red to red, see?" Or maybe *"C'est mon ami, Mademoiselle.* Yeah, I speak French. But not enough to hurt me. Ha ha!"

A cash investment at this point may help, as in "The tab? Ha ha, don't worry. I got it." Or "Take this Necco Wafer

ITTY BITTY MONKEY MAN

Certainly the earliest recorded sidekick. We know of "Itty Bitty Monkey Man," as he was dubbed by French archeologist Pierre LaPootre, thanks to a primitive charcoal drawing on a cave wall in an obscure cul-de-sac of the Lascaux Caves of southern France. There, amid 40,000-year-old renderings of mammoth hunts, saber-tooth tiger attacks, and swollen-bellied fertility symbols, is the unmistakable image of an heroic looking Cro-Magnon, apparently in full-throated song, while a grinning "itty bitty monkey man," tethered to his ankle by a cord, passes the hat.

"When I see this drawing on the cave wall, my heart, she stop, boom, like that," remembered LaPootre in a later interview. "I realize that here, in front of my eyes, is the first evidence of the sidekick dynamic. The first 'organ grinder and his monkey,' if you will. The first tiny step of the 40,000-year human journey that eventually brought us to Dean Martin and Jerry Lewis. I'm not ashamed to say I cry."

home to your little boy." Or "Do you know anybody who needs two tickets to the Elvis Resurrection? I've got Scouts that night." A little financial outlay now could translate into a lifetime of easy pickings at the trough.

Now seal the deal with a vision of a shared mission. "You're right! The world needs more whole life insurance policies!" Or "I'm with you on that. Somebody's gonna make a fortune, one widget at a time." Or maybe "Dreamers dream, but booty-kickers kick booty."

And never underestimate the power of the harmonica and a chorus of "Start spreading the news, I'm leaving today, I want to be a part of it, New York, New York . . . "

Congratulations, you enterprising sidekick, you. You've just found a hero! The hard part's done. Shift into maintenance mode, have a nice sandwich, and take the rest of the day off.

IT'S OKAY TO BE YOUR OWN SIDEKICK: A PUPPET PERSPECTIVE

Just for a moment, put yourself in a lonely hero's shoes. You need a sidekick. You've noticed that all great heroes have a sidekick and you want one too. But you're surrounded by henchmen, toadies, lackeys and minions. No one around you has the wit, the pluck, and the amusing hat and vocal

SIDEKICK SALUTE

BOB DENVER

Let us consider the inspiring example of Bob Denver.

Bob Denver—first as Maynard G. Krebs, sidekick to Dobie Gillis on *The Many Loves of Dobie Gillis*, and then as Gilligan, sidekick to an entire cast on the endlessly rerun *Gilligan's Island*—personified sidekick achievement: achievement made nobler because it never compromised the essence of what it means to be a sidekick.

No over-reaching for Bob Denver. No mistaking himself for a hero. No hissy fits in his trailer because "I should be doing Shakespeare in Central Park." Stardom, and an eponymous series, came to him precisely because he embraced his inner sidekick and let that bumbling, lovable laugh-getter loose on the audience.

A Sidekick Salute, then, to Bob Denver—double takes, vocal tics, wacky hat, big-eyed surprise reactions and all. You, sir, have set the bar!

mannerism to propel himself to sidekick status. Plus, who needs another expectant, open palm come payday?

The answer, my friend, may be as close as your foot. Take off a shoe. Remove a sock. Put your hand in the sock. Lift the sock up to your face and say, "Good morning, Mr. Sockus. How are you doing?"

Then scrunch up the toe part with your fingers, affect a nasally whine, and say, "Not bad, Mr. Hero. But I'm worried."

"Oh yeah?" you say. "Why?"

"'Cause this heel keeps following me! Ha ha ha!"

Presto! You've got a sidekick, and a cost-effective sidekick, at that. You've just had what psychologists call a "Buffalo Bob Moment," a shock of realization that a sidekick need not be on the payroll, indeed, need not be human.

Let's look at a few puppets who've blazed the sidekick trail:

HOWDY DOODY: Received star billing but functioned as sidekick to Buffalo Bob; beloved icon to a generation; proved that eleven strings connected to a block of wood can sell a lot of cereal.

FOZZIE BEAR: Quintessential sidekick and foil for Kermit the Frog; wacky hat; "Wocka wocka wocka" . . . need we say more?

CHARLIE McCARTHY: Radio and film star sidekick to Edgar Bergen; proved a witty enough sidekick makes it no problemo if the ventriloquist's mouth moves.

TOPO GIGIO: Not cost effective (it took three puppeteers plus a voice actor to animate the ten-inch foam mouse) but beloved worldwide; it's hard to argue with a sidekick who steals the show, says, "Eddie, keesa me goo' night!" and gets put back in a box.

JUDY: Descended from "Joan," a Neapolitan stock puppet character; wife and sidekick to Punch, an anti-hero whose outrageous, sometimes violent antics are part and parcel of Western culture. Judy broke new ground as an "anti-sidekick," that is, a sidekick who hits back.

JOHNNY: Talk about cost effective! Johnny consisted of two eyes and a mouth drawn in lipstick on Señor Wences' fist, accessorized with a tiny wig; another Wences sidekick—Pedro—was a disembodied head in a box, seen only once or twice a performance. Wences, a true genius of downsizing, carried an entire cast in a carry-on. Wences: "Is all right?" Pedro: "Is all right! Close the door."

You get the idea, Mr. or Ms. Hero. Put that fertile, aggressive, Type A brain to work! Pick up a sock, paint a face on a cantaloupe, invent an imaginary doofus who just left the room! Be your own sidekick! Let the others laugh! And then, charge them thirty bucks admission, twice a night.

"Strive not to be a success,
but rather to be of some value."

—Albert Einstein
to his sidekick "Sparky" (See page 101)

CHAPTER TWO

HOW TO BE A
SUCCESSFUL
SIDEKICK

THE ART OF THE SUPPORTIVE GUFFAW, AND MORE

FREDERICK DU FRENCH-BROAD

ROLE MODELS & INSPIRATIONS ★

Sidekick, translator, and nib whittler for Founding Father Benjamin Franklin. This witty sidekick (see "A Fool and his Frenchman are soon parted" in *Poor Richard's Almanack*) was credited by the prolific Franklin as "the fastest nib whittler in Philadelphia," and ". . . the only reason we got out of this Godforsaken town with a Document you could Read."

According to constitutional scholars, a shipment of limp quills and hopelessly dull nibs rendered early convention minutes, notes and drafts of the U.S. Constitution so much smeary gobbledegook. In an apocryphal anecdote that may or may not have happened, one memoir stated, " . . . the great inventor and Philosophe then cursed, flung the offending quill to the floor, and said, 'This wouldn't have happened under King George.'"

French-Broad, watching from the gallery, made his way to the convention floor, where he calmly picked up the offending quill, produced a Barlow knife from his vest pocket, and sharpened the nib to a perfect point in ten seconds. "Voila, Monsieur," he said, handing the quill back to Franklin, who tested it immediately on an amendment. "You, sir, have saved the Republic," said Franklin, and offered a "lunch and libation of thanksgiving" in gratitude.

From then on, the great Founding Father (and eventual Ambassador to France) and his beret-wearing, argyle-sporting, self-styled *sommelier* sidekick were rarely seen apart. Lively after-hours "midnight caucus" tavern conversations reputedly centered on physics, the "merits of French maidenhood," and the jovial French-Broad's assertion that "Hey, I need a Bill of Rights too. It is to laugh, yes? Ha ha." (*See Sidekick Bill of Rights, page 91.*)

(author's note: Curiously enough, French-Broad had no French ancestry. Birth records indicate he was born Richard Abraham Finebinder in Passaic, New Jersey, and adopted his Gallophile persona only after being struck by lightning while "Duck Hunting with a Rake," a popular drinking game in post-Revolution Philadelphia.)

ALL RIGHT, YOU'RE GETTING THE IDEA. THE Sidekick Way is looking like sweet relief from your unfulfilling, mind-numbing marathon in search of "achievement," whatever "achievement" means.

But what about the nuts and bolts, the meat on the bone, the inside scoop? Here are six rules, tips, and skills for sidekicks that must be followed. Or not.

SIDEKICK RULES

 **TRY HARD AT HARDLY TRYING**

Guidance counselors will never advise you to be a sidekick. Motivational speakers will never exclaim to you, "You're not quite good enough!" or urge you to "Settle for less than the best!" No, they say things like, "Be number one! Second best is for pathetic losers! Try hard, harder, and harder still until you rise to the top!" Well, that kind of thinking will never make you a sidekick.

No, as a future sidekick, when someone speaks to you like that you must come right back with, "Sir, I'm not thinking of being the best. I'm not thinking of trying hard, harder, and harder still! I'm not even thinking of trying *sorta* hard. Matter of fact, I'm thinking about hardly trying at all! My goal is to just rise somewhere in the vicinity of the top! In other words, my goal is to be a sidekick!"

 **FORGET PERSONAL DIGNITY**

You'd like to be a sidekick but you're worried about your personal dignity? Ha ha ha! You're not the first.

But here's the answer!

(An argument can be made that each member of the E Street Band has taken a turn as Springsteen's sidekick, which accounts, in part, for the longevity of that orchestra but we focus here on Little Steven.)

LITTLE STEVEN

Mick has Keith, Johnny had June, Sonny and Cher had each other, but for the tops in musical sidekicks we nominate Little Steven, a.k.a. Miami Steve Van Zandt.

Little Steven works slightly stage left of his boss, the Boss, adding guitar, mandolin, heartfelt harmony, and boundless upbeat support as the quintessential team player and sidekick.

Why? He's sidekick perfection, that's why. He has that odd *schmatta* for a wacky hat, the Jersey patois for a vocal tic, and an unswerving dedication to Bruce Springsteen's music and performance.

Meanwhile, he's carved a little piece of the show business pie for himself, as Silvio Dante, sidekick (what else?) to Tony Soprano. He's also the world's premier promoter of garage-band oddities and '60s rock 'n' roll on his Underground Garage franchise.

It's cliché, it's trite, and it's true: Little Steven, dude, you rock!

Check your dignity at the door . . . the door to peace, contentment, fulfillment, and happiness, marked "Sidekicks Enter Here!"

NEVER SAY NO TO THE HERO

Every hero has a posse. (Villains have gangs.) The members of the hero's posse are, for the most part, indistinguishable from each other. A sidekick is seldom *distinguished* but is never *indistinguishable*. Members of the posse are the ones who are toiling in the trenches, sweating the small stuff, and getting their boots muddy from the daily grind. A sidekick only gets his boots muddy when the hero does, and that's not very often. It's hard to look heroic when your boots are muddy.

However, on occasion, a hero will confuse his sidekick for a posse member and ask him to do something, like actually *work*. A sidekick never says no to the hero and he never says the obvious, which is, "Hey, big-shot hero, give that job to somebody in your posse!" No, the sidekick does just the opposite: he puts a big smile on his face and says, "I'm your man! Let me at 'em!" Then he jumps in feet first and royally screws it up. So badly that it's laughable. So badly that a posse member would have been fired for it.

Here's an example of very bad Hero thinking and the proper sidekick response.

HERO: "Okay ol' pardner, grab a shovel and dig us a latrine!"

The sidekick knows right off that neither shovel, dig, nor latrine, are in his job description, but he puts a big smile on his face and says "Let me at it!" Then he grabs a shovel and starts throwing dirt over his shoulder all over the hero, the hero's date, and even Cleveland if it's nearby.

HERO: "Whoa, pardner! Whoa! Whoa! Here give me that shovel! What was I thinking? Latrine, dig, and shovel aren't in your job description." Then the hero tosses the shovel to the posse and says "Here you guys, take care of the latrine. There's a good posse."

Yes, it was a job for the posse and the hero has properly blamed himself for sending his comic relief to do it. "I should've known better," he'll say with an embarrassed smile.

"Never send a sidekick to do the posse's job," the sidekick will reply with an easy grin. After this, the hero will never ask his sidekick to do that kind of work again. His sidekick can even volunteer and the hero will laugh it off. (When this happens, the sidekick should pretend to be upset about it and the hero will double his Christmas bonus.)

WHEN THE PIES FLY, TAKE 'EM. WHEN THE BULLETS FLY, FALL ON YOUR FACE.

Eventually a situation will arise when the sidekick can either pull the ripcord on his golden parachute or be stuffed in the corporate crapper and flushed from the bathroom of the big time. That's when the Sidekick Kicker comes in handy. It works like this:

ARTEMUS "SPEEDY" TREATORE

Sidekick to a bewildering variety of upper echelon officers in the American Civil War; gained notoriety at the Battle of Lickety Fiddle Spit when his aversion to blistering hot flying metal inspired a performance in the hundred-yard dash that one witness called "faster than the gol-durned *L&N* steam train goin' down the Owensboro grade. And buddy, that's fast!"

Sidekick scholars agree that Treatore set the standard for rapid attachment to a new hero. In one afternoon alone, in a skirmish near Carpel's Tunnel, Virginia, he began the battle as sidekick to General Amos Fitzhughe. Fitzhughe's demise came at roughly 1:10 p.m. By 1:14 p.m. Treatore was attached to Colonel Robert Smythe. Smythe passed into the Great Beyond at 1:27 p.m., and Treatore migrated to Major Lance. As his army's fortunes deteriorated, the intrepid Treatore worked his way down through captains, lieutenants, sergeants, and corporals, winding up that awful day as sidekick to one PFC Arnold Schapper.

Treatore assured himself of a plaque in the Sidekick Hall of Fame when Schapper died that night of shingles, and Treatore actually crossed enemy lines before dawn and attached himself to a regimental drummer for the OTHER side. His sub-sequent sidekick duties are recorded as nodding his head and saying to his new hero, as he sounded the marching cadence, "Yeah, man, that's a righteous groove," and loading snare drum cases onto an ox cart. Treatore is thus also recognized as history's first roadie.

The hero gets himself in big trouble (as heroes always do). The wagons are circled and someone has to slip through the enemy lines to bring back the cavalry. Whoever goes will probably be killed, mortally wounded, or captured and tortured. (Relax—as we shall see, none of these are a sidekick's job.)

The guys in the posse can't do it—they're all either too scared or too dead.

The hero won't do it. He has to stand there and look heroic in a big white hat while he grins in the face of danger.

So the hero turns his "grin in the face of danger" to the side-kick. The sidekick tries not to make eye contact. But it's no use. The sidekick is on the spot. He either volunteers to risk his life and limb, or he's not a sidekick, he's a coward. Alive, but a coward. Alive, but out of a job.

Time for the Sidekick "Kicker."

Time to save the day for the sidekick and leave the hero to get his own bacon out of the fire.

When the hero turns his "grin in the face of danger" on the sidekick, the sidekick steps up with his own big "grin in the face of danger" and volunteers to risk life and limb to ride for help. "I'm your man," he says. "Let me at 'em!" (Yes, this is the same thing the sidekick said just before he screwed up what should have been a member of the posse's job, and ought to be a clue to the hero, but this is not a problem. Heroes are generally too busy with the Big Picture to notice these little coincidences.) So, with a jaunty wave and a tip of his hat, the sidekick jumps on his mule, gallops into the jaws of death, and strategically falls on his butt before he gets in any real danger.

The sidekick risked nothing but a sore butt, and the hero will tear up over his Bombay Sapphire martini every time he recounts how his steadfast and loyal sidekick risked his life to save the hero's bacon. (See "Sidekick's Ace in the Hole," page 56, for a way to goose this kicker up a notch.)

The Sidekick "Kicker" also works when the hero looks to the sidekick to take a bullet for him. In this case, the sidekick

ELVIS' SIDEKICK
OR "THE SIDEKICK WHO NEVER WAS"

What's that? You don't acknowledge the sidekick's essential role? You think the world would be a better place without sidekicks messing up the plot, slowing the action for a joke, or humorously spilling something? Well, then, just consider Elvis. Poor Elvis.

It was lonely up there at the top. Sure, he had Priscilla, but she was too young and naive to understand and assuage his angst and pain. Sure, he had the Memphis Mafia and yes, they laughed at all his "jokes," but in the small, sad, scary hours before dawn, when the King was beset with insecurity and worry about lame movie roles and the British Invasion, they were worthless. In those awful, lonely moments, drugs made sense.

But what if "E" had had a sidekick to help him "TCB?" Somebody to hang with, somebody with an accent and a funny hat who wasn't there just to feed at the Presley trough, but was empowered to tease a little, lighten the mood, be a pal, and provide diversion and relaxation?

It could have all been different. Elvis could be with us today, not as a rumored sighting at Dunkin' Donuts, but as a cool rockin' daddy, incandescent on the stage, and making music that moves and matters.

We've been to Graceland, and we believe that next to the hallowed gravesites there's room for one more: an empty "Tomb of the Sidekick Who Never Was."

steps up, and just before the bullets fly, he stumbles over his own feet then rolls around on the ground trying to get up but only entangles himself in his feet even more. (For more detailed info on this maneuver, see the classic Carboni Stumble under "Tripping and Falling: Making Your Hero Look Good by Comparison, see page 62.")

SIDEKICK SALUTE

KATO

There are sidekicks who fall on their butts, there are sidekicks who somehow manage to kick their own butts, and then there was a sidekick named Kato, who, as played by martial arts legend Bruce Lee, simply kicked butt. Today hardly anyone remembers that Van Williams played the part of mild-mannered newspaper publisher Britt Reid, who secretly fought crime as the Green Hornet on television in the 1960s, but almost everyone knows that Bruce Lee played his kung fu valet sidekick, Kato.

Bruce Lee was born in San Francisco in 1940. His Chinese father was a well-known Cantonese opera and film actor who had brought his family with him on an extended tour of the United States. His mother was of German and Chinese ancestry.

When Bruce was three months old, his family returned to Hong Kong. He was a child actor in numerous Hong Kong–made movies.

As a teenager he became involved with a Chinese street gang. His father took him to a famous martial arts school with the idea of teaching him discipline and keeping him out of the gangs. Lee quickly became an expert at a variety of martial arts.

After high school he came to America, where he enrolled at the University of Washington as a philosophy major. He began to teach martial arts, and it was at an exhibition match in Los Angeles that he was spotted and signed to play the part of Kato in *The Green Hornet* television series. The show was a modest hit in America but a huge success in Hong Kong, where Bruce Lee as Kato received top billing. This led to his being signed to star in a Raymond Chow–produced kung fu movie called *Fists of Fury*.

By the time Lee completed making his third feature film, which he also directed, he was an international star. He died that same year of a brain edema believed to have been caused by a reaction to a prescription painkiller he was taking for back pain.

His career as a sidekick was short but unforgettable. He brought art, style, and ballet-like finesse to the world of sidekicks and managed to do all of this with a smile. We salute you, Bruce Lee, as the sidekick who literally put the "kick" in "sidekick!"

VILLAINS DO NOT HAVE SIDEKICKS

It might appear to the uninitiated that villains have side-kicks. No. Villains have accomplices, henchman, minions, and lackeys. These characters are mean, disloyal, brutal, and often psychotic. For the most part, they are in it for the money. They have no loyalty beyond their next payday and are generally ready to switch sides and betray their bosses at the drop of a bigger payoff. They are nothing more than thugs for hire and serve whomever will pay them for as long as the money holds out. They are, in turn, often betrayed, sent off to be killed, blamed for everything that goes wrong, smacked, whipped, and kicked. This is not a sidekick by any stretch of the imagination.

A sidekick may often be inept, bungling, and confused, but he is always loyal, lovable, kind, and never psychotic. Yes, he does expect to be paid or at least cut in on any rewards; but when times are rough, he stays by his hero's side no matter what and toughs it out. He never betrays his hero, and he is never whipped, smacked, or kicked.

HAVE A SIDEKICK ACE IN THE HOLE

What's an ace in the hole? Well, to be crass, it's something a sidekick has on the hero. Not something like a deep dark secret (see Sidekick's Golden Parachute); no, an ace in the hole is more like when the sidekick risked his all for the hero and fell off his horse trying. (See Sidekick Rule N°4.)

Once a sidekick gets an ace in the hole, he should never play it. A sidekick wouldn't be a sidekick if he did.

But from time to time (when he needs a raise or is up for a performance review), a sidekick might inadvertently let his hole card show. Maybe with a look of dejection on his face while mumbling something like, "This is the thanks I get for falling off my horse," or ". . . for tripping over my brogans trying to save you," or ". . . for dumping hot coffee on my head to cheer you up." There is no hero who on hearing these woe-filled words would not fail to heap praise and reward on his inept but faithful sidekick.

SIDEKICK SKILLS

It's hard to believe, but some people actually confuse side-kicks with layabout bums eager for a handout, a ham-mock, and a nice snooze; do-nothing loafers who lack the brainpower and moxie to get their foot in the correct pants leg. Not true. Successful sidekicks must have a repertoire of basic skills. Master these, friend, and drink deeply from the cup of contentment labeled "Sidekick Wine."

SIDEKICK
SALUTE

CHEWBACCA

When George Lucas created his Star Wars universe, he researched the work of Joseph Campbell, using mythical and cultural archetypes to inform his characters.

No wonder, then, that Chewbacca is an archetypal sidekick. Talk about wacky hair! His entire wardrobe is wacky hair. The guy is an eight-foot-tall Chia Pet.

Talk about a vocal tic! His entire verbal communication is a growling, strangled yodel, intelligible only to his hero, the perfectly coiffed space cowpoke Han Solo.

A good hand with a blaster, a gutsy co-pilot, a source of amusement, frustration and affection to his hero . . . what more do you want in a sidekick? We salute you, Chewie, and honor you with these immortal words of Wookie wisdom: "AaaaHRrrAAAaaHhhhh GRRRoooOOoorrwwWwggg AAAAAgggghHHHhcccCRaAAHaaaa!"

THE SUPPORTIVE GUFFAW

All right, say your hero cracks a joke, or what he THINKS is a joke. It's time for a Supportive Guffaw (see also Knowing Chuckle, Nervous Giggle, Uncomprehending Smirk, Wink-Wink Eyebrow Lift, Chagrined Grin, Gritted Teeth "Very Funny," and the "You-Got-Me-Ha-Ha-Ha").

What? You can't manage a Supportive Guffaw? No problem. The actual sound of the laugh isn't important. What matters is the "supportive" part. The sidekick must communicate to the hero that 1) it's a fine joke, 2) he's in on the joke, and 3) he stands ready to resuscitate the joke if it falls flat, even if it means the joke's on him.

For the gold standard of the Supportive Guffaw, look no further than Sidekick-Hall-of-Famer, if there were such a thing, Ed McMahon.

Aspiring sidekicks would do well to invest in old *Tonight Show* compilations, particularly the Ed/Karnak bits, for a glimpse of how it's done. The man was a genius. Just enough of a company man, just enough teasing of the hero, just enough comic timing to make the hero look better. And that laugh. It amused Johnny, it amused us, it saved countless routines that either weren't too funny to begin with or began petering out too soon.

For the post-modern ironic take on the Supportive Guffaw, we recommend studying Paul Shaffer. Shaffer proves you don't need a sincere laugh. In fact, you hardly need a laugh at all. You can get by with an attentive "Yeah," a knowing

5 AND ³/₈S-TUS

Sidekick, factotum, and "spiritual advisor" to Pope Sixtus IX.
5 and ³/₈s-tus' real name was Cardinal Guglio M. Carboni,
but he was well known to Vatican insiders by his nickname,
inspired by his diminutive stature. He perfected an amusing
fake stumble caused by catching one foot against the heel
of the other, a bit of physical comedy that lightened endless
late-night theological debates and brought tears of laughter
to the eyes of Sixtus IX. When papal duties became too
serious, the Pope often requested that his sidekick "pull a
Carboner." This turn of phrase transmogrified over the centuries into today's "pulling a boner."

nod that says, "I know there's a bad joke coming and I'm playing along because this is the best gig I've ever had," and a repetition of what the hero has just said.

EXAMPLE:

DAVID: "Paul, did you see this? A guy on the New Jersey Turnpike was stopped for having a car full of penguins."

PAUL: "Yeah, a car full of penguins." The grin. The nod. Now the hero knows he's not alone. Somebody else is in on the joke. Somebody has his back.

DAVID: "And when the patrolman told him to take them to the zoo, the guy said, 'I took 'em to the zoo yesterday. Today I'm taking them to the beach.'"

PAUL: "Aaahhh! Taking them to the beach!"

Grin. Nod. Play the break music. Pick up a nice check every two weeks. Ah, the sweet sidekick life!

TRIPPING AND FALLING: MAKING YOUR HERO LOOK GOOD BY COMPARISON

Never underestimate the power of a well-executed pratfall.

Careening into a file cabinet, banging your toe on a coffee table, or inexplicably stumbling on the way to the elevator are valuable weapons in the sidekick's arsenal.

We recommend the classic Carboni Stumble as a basic move. While walking normally, merely hook your right toe behind your left heel. The resulting falling and flailing will make you look like a fool and always amuse your hero.

figure a. Tripping and falling.

figure b. Wacky sneeze

You might also try the Wacky Sneeze, or the old Busted-Ink-Pen-in-the-Shirt-Pocket Gambit.

figure c. Walking into a pole

These maneuvers, not to mention walking into telephone poles, spit-takes, the old Finger-Stuck-in-the-Bottle Ruse, reinforce your position as a harmless, amusing mood lightener. The perfect companion for a hard-charging Type A personality.

figure d. The spit take

Judicious use of the pratfall can deflect unwanted attention from your hero during an awkward moment and ensure that the joke is properly centered on—who else—you, the sidekick.

EXAMPLE: You're in a tense meeting with your hero and the Mergers and Acquisitions Investigators from D.C. There seems to be some discrepancy between the sales numbers your hero reported for the last four years and actual inventory.

They're asking pointed questions, using phrases like, "What did you know and when did you know it?" and "Do you realize bail is out of the question?"

You say, "Anybody for coffee?" You get up, cross towards the bagel and coffee tray, and go into a Carboni Stumble, pulling the whole thing down on you in a hilarious mess.

When the laughter finally dies down, and your hero says, "Let's get the cleaning staff in here . . . again!", and more laughter. The Feds may say, "Oh heck, let's wrap this thing up. We've got a plane to catch. Looks like your figures are close enough for government work. Ha ha ha."

Good work! You might be looking at a Sidekick Bonus!

ROLE
MODELS &
INSPIRATIONS
★

JONATHAN, EARL OF DEBBINGTON

Trusted personal assistant and sidekick to Elizabeth I; known to the Queen as "Debbie;" met the future monarch when both attended summer youth theater camp run by then struggling playwright William Shakespeare.

"Debbie's" passion for exotic stage makeup resulted in his revolutionary "white on white on white," or "explosion in the marshmallow factory" look, which Elizabeth adopted for everyday life.

No marital records exist for the Earl of Debbington, and he is widely credited with originating the old saying "One Queen in my life is plenty, thank you."

BY JOVE, HOLMES, HOW IN BLAZES DID YOU EVER DEDUCE THAT?

CLASSIC SIDEKICK COMPLIMENTS: WHEN "GREAT IDEA, BOSS!" JUST ISN'T ENOUGH

When today's sidekick needs to compliment her hero, she has a treasure trove of the classics to choose from. Feast your eyes and adapt as needed.

GABBY HAYES: "Nice piece of shootin', Roy."

MR. SPOCK: "Highly illogical, Captain, but effective."

ETHEL: "Gosh, Lucy, that was great. Say, I bet you could win Ricky's talent show!"

BARNEY: "How'd you know, Andy?"

FALSTAFF: "I shall think the better of myself, and thee, during my life—I for a valiant lion, and thou for a true prince."

TONTO: "That right, Kimosabe."

SANCHO PANZA: "How much does honor pay by the hour?"

SILENT BOB: "_____"

SAMWISE GAMGEE: "I wonder if people will ever say, 'Let's hear about Frodo and the Ring.' And they'll say, 'Yes, that's one of my favorite stories. Frodo was really courageous, wasn't he, Dad?' 'Yes, my boy, the most famousest of hobbits. And that's saying a lot.'"

RON WEASLEY: "There you go, Harry. You weren't being thick after all—you were showing moral fiber!"

DEVELOP A SPECIALTY

Sidekicks in it for the long haul have what smart people like us call a "specialty." You're probably thinking, *A specialty? What the heck do I need with a specialty? I'm a sidekick, for crying out loud.*

Don't fall into the old trap of believing that the sidekick life means you don't have to do anything. That's not a sidekick. That's a shiftless lie-abed. (If you care to write a book called *The Official Shiftless Lie-abed Handbook,* we salute you.)

A specialty can endear you to a hero, particularly if it's doing something the hero would rather not—or can't—do himself, and insures that you don't fall into the dreaded "toadie" category (see Common Sidekick Pitfalls). Plus, if your hero

MYAH WHEW

Court adjutant of the tumultuous Middle Whang Dynasty; credited with first use of "Bloom where you're planted"; managed a lifelong, profitable career as sidekick to a bewildering succession of emperors and heads of state in a time of assassinations, suicides, beheadings, and torture. Famous for his relentlessly upbeat attitude, optimistic turns of phrase (he's also acknowledged as the author of "Hey, it could be worse. It could be raining!"), and natural chameleon skill of turning into the wallpaper.

FRED AND ETHEL

Let us salute Vivian Vance and William Frawley, sidekicks who would be in the inaugural class of The Sidekick Hall of Fame, if there were such a thing.

Stalwart second bananas to Lucille Ball and Desi Arnaz, these masters of comic timing helped propel *I Love Lucy* into American cultural iconography.

And, in TV-land, they were married! Think of it! Sidekicks who were not only married, but functioned as sidekicks to a couple of heroes who were also married! So, you had four-way scenes of heroine/sidekick playing against hero/side-kick. The possibilities boggle the mind: Lucy and Ethel, Lucy and Fred, Ricky and Ethel, Ricky and Fred, and then all the concomitant groups of three. It was the comedic mother lode, and the show's writers took full advantage.

Ethel and Fred, take your solo bows!

falls on hard times, or you're between heroes, it's good to be able to pull in a paycheck until the next hero comes along.

What skills are we talking about? Let's look at Fred, Desi's sidekick. Fred was quite a handyman, fixing minor plumbing and electrical foul-ups, painting, washing windows. He could also execute a vaudeville soft-shoe routine if needed. This 'specialty set' kept him close to his hero and fully employed. Improvise, use what you've got, and access your inner Fred.

OTHER TIME-TESTED SIDEKICK SPECIALTIES: make-up artist, bartender, cook, interpreter, fisherman (see "New Testament Sidekicks"), witty conversationalist, sports handicapper, gold prospector (see "Classic Cowboy B-movie Sidekicks"), diarist, golfer/caddy, semi-proficient harmonica player (see "Polly Wolly Doodle"), eBay expert, dog walker, movie critic, driver, amateur historian, trivia expert, masseuse, etc.

THE ANNOYING SIDEKICK

A strange dichotomy is that of the hero and the annoying sidekick. Why on earth would anyone, let alone a hero, put up with a sidekick like Jar Jar Binks or J. Wellington Wimpy? Well, the secret to success for the annoying sidekick is not much more than proximity, helplessness, and pity—three powerful forces that combine to bond together a hero and a pain in the ass. In other words, a sidekick's total worthlessness brings out the big brother in the hero.

TIPS FOR BEING AN ANNOYING SIDEKICK:

★ When it comes to cologne, it's never enough.

★ Cultivate a high-pitched whiny voice.

★ Never miss a chance to borrow money to buy a hamburger on Tuesday.

★ Three words: clingy, needy, nerdy.

★ Stick your nose where it doesn't belong.

★ Always be either giggling, bitching, or moaning.

★ Shriek and gasp whenever anything happens, whether it's good or bad.

★ Speak in rhymes.

CONSTANTLY USE THESE ANNOYING WORDS AND PHRASES:

★ Whatever.

★ It's all good.

★ Can we talk?

★ Shut your pie hole.

★ You know what you should do?

★ It is what it is.

★ My bad.

★ Everything happens for a reason.

★ You know?

★ You rock.

★ Dude.

CHAPTER THREE

SEVEN HABITS

OF HIGHLY SUCCESSFUL SIDEKICKS

INSPIRING SECRETS OF THE GREAT ONES

BOOKS LIKE THIS ONE NEEDS SHORT, SNAPPY memorable lists of things everybody knows. Here is ours: seven habits that are second nature to the wise sidekick, and the building blocks of a fruitful sidekick career.

1 Never have better hair than your hero.

Incorrect.

CORRECT!

2 Talk sports. Talking sports is what buddies do. How did your hero's team fare last weekend? No clue? Fake it with "How about that call?" or "That was some defense!" or the ever popular "What a finish!"

No.

YES!

3 Become one with the wallpaper. If your hero has an awkward or embarrassing moment, you disappear, only to pop up again with a zany quip. Example: "Whoa! Where did THAT load of bushwa come from? Ha ha."

Can you spot the sidekick here?

4 Be the butt of the joke. Knowing two or three jokes is good (see *Milton Berle's Private Joke File*), but make sure the joke's on you.

Unsuitable.

SELF-EFFACING!

5 Avoid the spotlight. If you just can't help it and the spotlight shines on you, fall into the horse trough.

Hogging the spotlight.

COMIC RELIEF!

Not sidekick attire.

6 Sidekick wardrobe: Hawaiian shirts are your friends. They are the great levelers. Wacky hats are a must.

ATTA BOY!

GREAT IDEA

Merely supportive.

7 Practice saying "great idea!" It must be sincere. Once you can fake sincerity, you've got it made.

GREAT IDEA!

OUT OF THE PARK!

SMILEY BURNETTE

Lester Alvin "Smiley" Burnette was the first to popularize the comic cowboy sidekick. He was also one of the best and most beloved, and for fourteen years he ranked higher than all but a few of the cowboy stars themselves in box office popularity polls. He was the only cowboy sidekick ever to get top billing in a western series—over the cowboy hero Sunset Carson. He was a multi-instrumentalist who wrote hundreds of songs, mostly novelties like "Elmer the Absent-minded Cowboy" and "The Defective Detective from Brooklyn," but also including the beautiful western classic "Riding Down the Canyon."

His career started when he joined up with Gene Autry as an accordion player on the WLS *National Barn Dance* radio program and soon became Gene's comic radio sidekick. A year later they both headed to Hollywood, where Smiley basically created the comic cowboy sidekick in dozens of western movies. After he showed 'em how it was done and how much fun it added to the movie, there would be very few westerns made without the hero having a comic sidekick. After appearing in over a hundred movies, including several non-westerns, where he sidekicked up with the likes of Dick Tracy, Rin Tin Tin, and Ray "Crash" Corrigan, Smiley went on to costar in the top ten–rated television show *Petticoat Junction*. Smiley is a member of the Cowboy Hall of Fame and the Nashville Songwriter Hall of Fame and is scheduled to be one of the first inductees into our new Sidekick Hall of Fame. We salute you, Smiley, and in the words of your long-time friend Gene Autry, you were "a sweet and easygoing fellow, and best of all, you made us laugh."

"The doctor X-rayed my head
and found nothing."

—Arkansas Slim,
sidekick to Tex Ritter

CHAPTER FOUR

TRAPS & PITFALLS

WHAT A SIDEKICK ISN'T

STAND TALL, MR. AND MS. SIDEKICK! YOU HAVE rights. You can demand stuff. Go ahead and do it! We're right behind you! Way back here, out of the line of fire, about where you'd find a . . . can you guess? That's right! A sidekick!

WHEN HEROES CROSS THE LINE

It happens from time to time that a hero turns out to have feet of clay and violates the hero code, as well as state and federal anti-racketeering laws. When this happens it's important for the sidekick to know the difference between a supportive relationship and aiding and abetting. A few moments spent reviewing recent RICO indictments might save a sidekick a big headache, say one that lasts 10 to 15 years with time off for good behavior.

Extricating yourself from a potentially criminal situation could be just as simple as easing out the back door, maybe tossing in a pratfall just to show that you're too dim to be of interest.

If this doesn't work and you're called to testify, plead lovable incompetence, then give the court a goofy grin as you take a drink of water and let it dribble down the front of your shirt.

A WINGMAN IS NOT A SIDEKICK

"Wingman" is a word that has come into recent usage and should not be confused with "sidekick." *Wingman* originally was a term coined by the military to designate the pilot that flies slightly behind and apart from the leader in a flight formation. His job is to cover the leader's back in aerial combat. The term entered popular usage and took on a whole new meaning after it was used in the movies *Top Gun* and *Swingers*, and in a popular Coors Light television commercial. The wingman in this sense of the word is a guy whose job it is to approach a pair of females in a bar or other such setting and engage the less desirable female of the two in a conversation. His buddy than walks over and the two men act like they just ran into each other, and this leads to introductions all around. The baloney starts to get sliced pretty thick as the wingman goes along with any lies the other guy tells and generally extols his talents and makes him look better than Brad Pitt and George Clooney rolled into one.

So, is a wingman a sidekick? Not on your sweet banana peel pratfall. A wingman is more like an accomplice who makes his buddy look good by feigning affection to some unfortunate woman and by going along with his buddy's lies. A sidekick makes the hero look good because the sidekick looks so bad, so funny, so lovably inept—and nobody gets lied to or used in the process.

You are a sidekick. Embrace your fate. Follow your lower calling and bloom where you're planted, right next to a star.

THE BUSH 43 PITFALL: WHEN SIDEKICKS OVERREACH

Sidekicks must beware of temptation. The fleeting glitter, glamour and so-called perks of stardom will beckon. Seeing a Star in action, up close and personal, is sure to provoke the all-to-human response, "Hell's bells, I could do THAT." Of course you could—anybody could. But don't take the bait. It will just lead you to endless, meaningless work and worry, not to mention your incompetent bumbling, which could jeopardize everyone in sight as you try to be something you're not.

History is lousy with Overreaching Sidekicks and their gifts of missing the point, interfering, and screwing up the deal for everybody else.

Consider George W. Bush. Here was a guy universally considered to be a fine fellow, a regular Joe, a down-to-earth hail-fellow-well-met. Surveys repeatedly named him the best president to have a beer with. He was quick with a teasing nickname, he kept things light with absurd syntax, and he could talk sports. In short, a sidekick.

But something happened along the way. Whether *hubris* or backroom manipulation gets the blame, we'll let history decide. But W. woke up one morning in the driver's seat of the Free World, where he—and much of the Free World—seemed uneasy. He had overreached.

He began to say things like, "I'm the commander, see? I don't need to explain . . . I do not need to explain why I say things. That's the interesting thing about being president."

He clearly knew there was a problem and tried to articulate it the best he could: "I don't particularly like it when people put words in my mouth, either, by the way, unless I say it."

Until finally, to a pretty universal sense of relief, he summed up his legacy of good, bad, and debatable governance with, "I think we agree, the past is over."

These days W. is . . . in his own words . . . "following Barney (his dog) around the neighborhood with a plastic bag on my hand," two-stepping with Laura in the kitchen, and cracking a cold cola before the big game. He's back to being a sidekick, and we'd bet the ranch he'll tell you he's mighty glad of it.

Learn his lesson well. You are a Sidekick. Embrace your fate. Follow your lower calling and bloom where you're planted, right next to a Star.

SMALL RA

Earliest known administrative assistant; employed in the court of Pharaoh Tutankhamen IX, famously derided as the "Three Blocks Shy of a Pyramid" Pharaoh. Recently decoded hieroglyphics indicate Small Ra was present at many court "shizzles," or "parties," with no apparent function other than to amuse and agree with King Tut IX. One newly excavated fragment seems to show Small Ra reclining on a pleasure barge, nodding as if to say, "Great idea, Pharaoh!"

SIDEKICK BILL OF RIGHTS

Workman laboring far beneath the streets of Philadelphia, excavating a subterranean parking structure, recently unearthed a musty iron-and-leather-bound trunk. All construction was halted immediately, as scholars from The Serling-Franklin Institute were notified. Dr. Carlos "Hap" Mendoza, leader of the archeological team sent to investigate, oversaw the opening of the trunk.

"It was crammed to the brim with Revolutionary-era boxer shorts and socks," reported Mendoza. "Some original Betsy Ross argyle. Those alone made it priceless. But the real payoff was on the bottom, wrapped around what looked like the remains of a Reuben sandwich. I unrolled the parchment with trembling hands and beheld . . . the Sidekick Bill of Rights."

This document, apparently the result of the fabled Opal's Tap Room "midnight caucus sessions" of the Constitutional Convention, and long the subject of rumor and speculation, can now take its rightful place in American history.

Here, for the first time, thanks to the Freedom of Sounds Weird But Might Be Plausible Information Act, is the Sidekick Bill of Rights.

*W*e, the SIDEKICKS *of the United States of America*, in order to FORM A MORE PERFECT PARCHMENT, ESTABLISH SOME DANG RULES, and ENSURE THE DOMESTIC SUPPLY OF HOPS AND BREW, do HEREBY DECLARE the SIDEKICK BILL OF RIGHTS. These Amendments shall be Appended to the Constitution now under Advisement, but if, and Only if, I Finish this Sandwich. Wait . . . I'll be There in a Minute . . .

1. We hold this Truth to be Self-Evident: That if a SIDEKICK be required to Comickly fall off a Horse or Mule into a Horse Trough, the Trough shall be filled with water heated to at least 74 degrees Fahrenheit, but not more than 103 degrees Fahrenheit. *(See Hot Tub Exclusion Clause.)*

2. If, when in the course of SIDEKICK Events, it becomes necessary for a SIDEKICK to receive a Pie in the Face, it must be an Agreeable Custard of Suitable Vintage. No fruit Fillings or Nastie Compotes will be Tolerated.

3. A clean glass of Water will be provided to the SIDEKICK at the beginning of each day's Work so he'll have Someplace to keep his false Teeth while in Character.

4. The SIDEKICK shall have access to all Picnicking and Catering and shall be allowed normal Seating. However, unusually Rank or disgusting SIDEKICKS will be provided with a shaded Area and lawn Chair not beyond a maximum of 250 feet downwind from the Buffet Tables.

5. The SIDEKICK shall enjoy the Fruits of his Labors, Respect from his Peers, and a Benefits Package commensurate with his Seasons of Service.

6. The SIDEKICK gets to Vote, but it doesn't mean Anything.

7. The SIDEKICK's vocal Tic or trademark bit of Physickal Business shall be deemed his Alone, and no other SIDEKICK may use it, unless he reimburses the Original SIDEKICK with a royalty Payment to be determined by Privy Council. (*See Council in the Privy.*)

8. Should a SIDEKICK execute a *Fall de la Prat*, he shall Receive immediate medical Attention, once the Laughter has Died Down.

9. SIDEKICK shall be afforded equal Protection Under the Law, without Regard to Race, Gender, or Political Opinion, unless He's such a Goofball it doesn't Matter. (*See Goofball Exclusion.*)

10. The SIDEKICK shall be Awarded, in Perpetuity, a Generous Allowance of Intoxicants, to be Paid for by the Gentleman from Suffolk over There in the Corner.

THE LONE RANGER AND TONTO DISCUSS TONTO'S BENEFITS PACKAGE

A heretofore unknown acetate recording has surfaced from the basement of the prestigious "Brace Beemer Archives." It apparently documents a conversation between the Lone Ranger and his "Faithful Indian Companion" and sidekick, Tonto.

CHAPTER FIVE

SIDEKICK SUCCESSION

THE DELICATE NUANCES
OF ATTACHING YOURSELF
TO A NEW HERO WHEN
THE OLD ONE IS FIRED

MAYBE YOU SAW IT COMING, OR MAYBE IT'S A bolt out of the blue: your hero goes down. Down, as in fired, pink-slipped, kaput, "You're out of here, Buddy, and, by the way, legal proceedings start Monday morning."

You're an unemployed sidekick, and that's not good. You're a Moon without an Earth, which makes you an asteroid. And asteroids are never good news, wandering around by themselves in crazy orbits. Keep in mind Sir Humphrey Davy's immortal verse, "Beware!":

> Beware! and shun the Asteroid
> Collision-bound, and unemployed.

You've got to move on, and the sooner the better. Oh sure, you can hang out with your former hero for a half hour or so, maybe commiserate over a couple of Harvey Wallbangers, but beware the descent into Confessor Country, Wronged Best-Friendville, or the dreaded Land of the Vindictive.

These pits of emotional quicksand must be avoided. The only way to look at your past hero is in the rear-view mirror. A handshake, a "Hey, life gives you lemons, you make lemonade. Right, Bucko?" a tip of your wacky hat, and you are out the door, down the hall, and on the trail of a new hero.

A bit of subtlety is in order. It won't do to simply ease up to the cubicle of the boss's son-in-law and announce, "It's about time they trimmed some dead wood out of this place. Hey, pal, had lunch yet?"

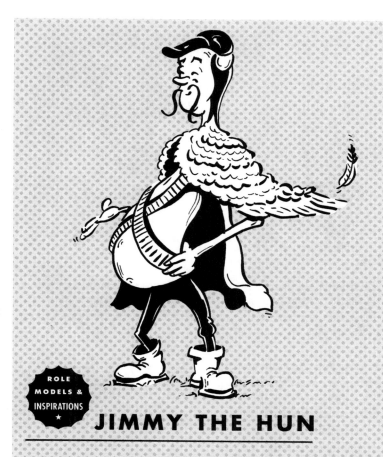

JIMMY THE HUN

Attila's second in command—although there is no record of his ever "commanding" anything—Jimmy the Hun apparently struck the dour, power-crazed Attila as funny, having perfected a zany hitch in his step that always lightened the mood around the yurt after a tough day of pillaging. We know of the "Fun Hun" today thanks to tall tales handed down through the centuries and his celebration in children's folk songs, such as, "Here comes Jimmy, here comes fun, walks like a goose, that's one funny Hun."

BARNEY FIFE

The tires of his '64 Ford Galaxy cop car squealing to a stop, he leaps out onto the sidewalks of Mayberry, brandishing his unloaded revolver wildly, overreacting, missing the point, and defining true sidekick sensibility.

Barney Fife, brought to unforgettable life by Don Knotts, with his voice cracking to a pre-pubescent falsetto and his skinny limbs flailing, must be in anyone's pantheon of Top Five TV Sidekicks.

Imagine Andy without Barney. There he sits, feet up on his desk, affably overseeing his town's citizenry, parenting Opie, complimenting Aunt Bea's cooking, and that's about it. Pretty dull there in Mayberry with no nincompoop racing in with garbled news of crooks headed their way, no mistaken identity gambits, and no screwing up of Andy's carefully laid plans amid the minefield of small town social politics.

We salute old One Bullet Barney Fife. Like all the great sidekicks, it just ain't a show without him.

No, that would be slimy, and sidekicks aren't slimy. Sidekicks are sincere, and as we all know, once you can fake sincerity, you've got it made.

It's important to remember that everybody knows of your previous, just concluded, relationship. It's no good pretending it never happened. "What am I doing here? Was it all a nightmare? Thank God I woke up!" though tempting, won't cut it.

SPARKY

Einstein's sidekick. Never got the press his boss did; seldom photographed but often seen at the great physicist's side, roaming the Princeton campus. Sparky, last name unknown, is responsible for iconic image of Einstein sticking out his tongue in the famous photograph. Just as the photographer was about to snap the shutter, Sparky reportedly said, "So, Al, what's the 'c' in E=mc squared stand for? Coleslaw? Ha ha ha!" Often, when Einstein relaxed with his violin, Sparky accompanied him on harmonica in a raucous version of "Polly Wolly Doodle."

A surer path to new horizons is to let it be known that you're really not all that surprised he was let go. And it's no big deal. "Yeah, we were pretty good friends, but he was getting into some stuff that seemed a little sketchy." Use the power of non-specific innuendo and the slight, knowing "What are you gonna do?" shrug to separate yourself from your "friend."

Got it? Great! You're a free agent. Now, it's Square One time. (See "Tips on Finding a Hero.") But you'll never find a hero hanging out by yourself in pachinko parlors. You don't hunt lions in a laundromat, Mr. Sidekick-at-Liberty. You've got to go where the prey is—the hotel bar after a tough day's video conference, the first tee, the boss's birthday bash, any semi-social work environment where your side-kick skills can shine. (See "Ingratiation.")

Go get 'em, Mr. First Companion Among Equals! Today is The Day! This is The Place! You are The Guy!

THE FUNNY KATO/CATO

In the 1964 movie *A Shot in the Dark,* the inimitable Peter Sellers played bumbling Inspector Jacques Clouseau, and Burt Kwouk played his manservant/sidekick Kato Fong. (Kwouk's funny Kato was modeled after Bruce Lee's serious Kato in the TV series *The Green Hornet.*) In addition to looking after

Clouseau's household, Kato's job was to leap out of closets or from behind curtains without warning and attempt to beat Clouseau to a pulp. This was Clouseau's idea, and its purpose was to keep him always on his guard and in "fighting trim." Both characters were experts at martial arts and their battles routinely resulted in the destruction of furniture, dishes, chandeliers, and other household items. The battles usually ended when the phone rang or there was a knock at the door and Kato had to stop fighting and resume his valet duties. (This was as funny as it sounds.) The movie was a success and there were a number of sequels, though in the subsequent films the spelling of "Kato" was changed to "Cato."

Burt Kwouk was born in Manchester, England, in 1930 and raised in Shanghai. He appeared in over sixty movies and dozens of television shows. But to many he will always be remembered and saluted as the wonderful and funny Kato/Cato.

SCARABETTRA

Cleopatra's gal-pal; earliest recorded distaff sidekick and makeup artist; invented influential "bangs with a bob" hairstyle and apparently advised Cleopatra on matters of the heart, approving a suitor with "Here comes Old Mister Obelisk," or rejecting him as "croc-worthy" and booting him off the barge.

Legal scholars credit her with origination of the "Egyptian Escape," a maneuver still used in contentious probate negotiations. Her reputation as legal innovator is supported by newly translated Aswan papyri documents recording Cleopatra's last conversation with Scarabettra.

CHAPTER SIX

WHEN A SIDEKICK NEEDS A SIDEKICK

SIDEKICKS & MARRIAGE

LET'S FACE IT, FEW PEOPLE DREAM OF WAKING up every morning next to a second banana.

It doesn't mean they're bad, or particularly ignorant; it just means that they've succumbed to the cultural tsunami that insists "Number 1 equals success, every other number equals failure." It's time to stand up to this ruinous "top of the heap" mind-set!

COURTSHIP RITUALS

Say you meet a stranger who would make a desirable companion. If they're still talking to you after noticing your wacky hat, you have a chance. Go for it! Speak in an amusing dialect, embellished with a zany vocal tic. Don't forget the power of gibberish!

Access is an advantage. Relate a tantalizing detail about your Star, something only you, in your role as sidekick, could know. Not too tantalizing, of course. After all, you're not looking for a desirable companion for the Star, now are you?

Still talking? Great! Now cook the object of your fascination a meal. Turn the conversation to scientific studies correlating low cholesterol with low sidekick stress. Mention heart-healthy aspects of letting somebody else lose sleep since they were passed over for the Albuquerque promotion.

Emphasize that you are not drifting aimlessly through life, a goofy wayward ship without a rudder. On the contrary, you have made a reasonable, informed career choice to follow a rewarding path of less resistance. And it's fun. And you get to wear a wacky hat. And you need . . . and here's the clincher . . . a sidekick!

Difficult as it may be to believe, this won't always work. There are hard cases out there that will just think you're a pitiable idiot and move on to more "promising" prospects, whatever "promising " means.

But, lucky for you, there is a fine pool of prospective "sidekicks for sidekicks" who will think you're so cute, so funny, and so smart to step aside and let the other rats race by that they'll gladly embrace you and your destiny.

They'll see you not as a lazy screw-up, but as you really are: a visionary. Then all you have to do is start remodeling for the baby's room.

"The congressman hung
around after the Voter's League
town hall meeting to discuss the high
cost of living with several women."

—**Robert "Skip" Patey,**
*inarticulate former sidekick to a
former Southern congressman*

CHAPTER SEVEN

SIDEKICK

ARCHETYPES

PATTERN YOUR LIFE AFTER THESE INSPIRING EXEMPLARS

THESE SIDEKICK ARCHETYPES POINT THE WAY.
Study them, quietly meditate on which of their singular characteristics you can add to your own life, and then take action. Somewhere in the sidekick universe there is a wacky hat with your name on it. Claim it, my friend, place it on top of your odd, wispy hair, say something in gibberish, and set your inner sidekick free.

SIDEKICK HEAVEN

An argument can be made that the apotheosis of the Sidekick Ethos was manifested in the B Westerns of the 1930s and '40s, in the films of heroes like Roy Rogers, Gene Autry, Tex Ritter, et al.

Images of their sidekicks, those crusty, loyal, humorous, eccentric scene-stealers define what many of us think of when we hear the word "sidekick."

Sure, the music of the singing cowboys was wonderful, but generations of pint-sized moviegoers couldn't wait for the warbling to stop so that Gabby and Frog and Fuzzy could get back onscreen and cut-up and fall into the horse trough. They made us laugh and they kept the plot moving, and really, what more is there?

Riders In The Sky, a Grammy-winning musical quartet, is keeping vintage Western music alive and kicking, and, of course, they have a sidekick, their cook, the beloved . . . well, tolerated . . . Sidemeat.

Sidemeat, with his turned-up hat, greasy apron and trademark vocal tic "Myah whew!" often appears on the Riders' show, billed as "The Only Western Sidekick Currently Making a Living."

Here, transcribed verbatim from a rare "live" recording of Riders In The Sky at the Kentucky State Fair's prestigious Hall of Giant Vegetables, is Sidemeat's signature performance of his beloved . . . well, tolerated . . . "I Dreamed I Was There in Sidekick Heaven."

(As you read this transcript, imagine a mush-mouthed, gibberish-inflected voice. Myah whew!)

CUE THE MUSIC: *I dreamed I was there in Sidekick Heaven*

Oh, what a beautiful sight!

I don't know if it was that foot-long green chili burrito I got down at the Shoot 'n' Scoot or what, but boys, I had a heckuva dream last night.

I dreamed I rode my old mule Senator, up through the clouds and clean as far as Sidekick Heaven. I rode him right through them big pearly corral gates they got up there and tied him up at a diamond hitchin' post.

And then I seen him! Leanin' against the bunkhouse door, waitin' to greet me! It was the greatest Sidekick of 'em all: **Gabby Hayes!**

Gabby looks at me with a toothless grin and says, "Eshewah eshewah eshewah, Sidemeat. Eshewah eshewah eshewah shewah?"

"What the heck did you say?" I says. "Can't you speak English so's a man can unnerstan' ya?"

He said "Myah whew!" And I knew he wanted me to come inside!

CUE THE MUSIC: I dreamed I was there in Sidekick Heaven

Oh, what a star-studded night.

We walked into the bunkhouse and there they was, sittin' at a barrel playin' poker, a couple of the Fuzzys, **Fuzzy Knight** and **Al "Fuzzy" St. John.** Howdy boys!

And sittin' over there by the stove, whittlin', there's **Pat Buttram** and **Cannonball Taylor!**

And leanin' against the wall, givin' me a wink, **Walter Brennan!** "One a these days I'm gonna climb that mountain," he says, just like in the song. "I guess you climbed it all right, Walter," I says back at him.

And then I sees a couple guys over in the corner: **Tonto!** "Hmmm, Kimosabe." And **Pancho!** "Oh ho, Ceesco!"

And way in the corner there, servin' up beans and biscuits, it was **Hop Sing!** I reckon that was the Third World Corner of Sidekick Heaven.

Then I hears a great commotion and I looks out the window and there, drivin' a jeep and yelling "Whoa, Nellie Belle, Whoa!" It was **Pat Brady!**

CUE THE MUSIC: I dreamed I was there in Sidekick Heaven

Oh, but their timing was great.

We walked out the back door and I seen him fall off his horse into the horse trough, just like he did in five thousand Gene Autry pictures: **Smiley Burnett.** Old "Frog Millhouse."

And there, galloping across the plains and hollerin' "Wait for me, Wild Bill, wait for me!" It was **Andy Devine.**

Then I seen a bunch of guys sittin' on the top rail of the corral fence. They kinda looked familiar but I didn't know who they was. Then it hit me. It was "The Sidekicks That No One Can Remember."

Raymond Hatton! Who would know Raymond Hatton? I didn't know him. He had a little name tag that said "Hello, I'm Raymond Hatton. Welcome to Sidekick Heaven. Have a nice day."

Next to him was **Arkansas Slim Andrews**. And **Emmet Lynn**. And **Roscoe Ates**. And **Max Terhune** and **Little Elmer.** And they'd SWITCHED their name tags! I tell ya, it's always somethin' up there in Sidekick Heaven. Myah whew!

Then the old Gabbaroo says, "C'mon, Sidemeat. Let's go up to the Big Boss's Ranch House. There's somethin' there I believe you'd like to see."

And he took me into a beautiful golden room, with a beautiful golden light comin' down, and you couldn't tell where it was comin' from. And all you could hear was a guitar. And an accordion. And a fiddle, playin' way up high. Way up there. And it was in tune! That's how I knowed it was heaven.

Gabby picks up this big Tally Book, and blows off some gold dust, and turns the pages, and written there in . . . I don't know . . . pure platinum or somethin' . . . they don't cut no corners in Sidekick Heaven . . . was the names of all the sidekicks!

Then Gabby says, "And here's the names of all the fellers yet to come to Sidekick Heaven." And he starts to read. **"Little Beaver,** played by Robert Blake, **Joe Biden** . . . "

Joe Biden? He's gonna need a name tag.

And then he says, **"Sidemeat** . . . " Sidemeat????!!!!!!! Myah whew! And that's when I awoke. And I'm sorry I did.

CUE THE MUSIC: *'Cause I dreamed I was there in Sidekick Heaven*

Oh, what a beautiful sight.

Save me a plate o' beans, boys (wiping away a tear). I'm on my way. Myah whew!

LENNY "THE STOOGE OF OMAHA"

Leonard R. Kaplough (pronounced "Kap-lough"): trusted aide and confidant of billionaire stock investor Warren Buffet. This little known and seldom written about sidekick to "The Sage of Omaha" apparently came from humble beginnings as the son of the curator of the Fort Dodge Wrestling Hall of Fame. Making Buffet's acquaintance while dispensing soft-serve treats at an Omaha Dairy Queen, "Lenny," as he's known to Buffet, saw the potential of the then youthful, intense security analyst, offered a "double dip swirl . . . with nuts, on the house—a nice dividend, hey?" and cemented a sidekick/ hero relationship that's withstood global financial meltdowns, market upheavals, and golf with Bill Gates.

The only living person who can get away with calling his hero "Buffay, you know, like the lunch," Lenny's pitch-perfect impression of all Three Stooges in the "Calling Dr. Howard, Calling Dr. Fine" sketch reliably reduces one of The World's Richest Men to gasping laughter. It was the witty Buffet him- self who, after one such interlude at a private stock evalua- tion conference, dubbed Kaplough "The Stooge of Omaha."

WESTERN SIDEKICK

Reached popular zenith in 1930s and '40s B Westerns.

SALIENT CHARACTERISTICS: dusty hat turned up in front, greasy apron, wispy facial hair, crusty winter underwear peeking out from under shirt, teeth optional, trademark tic or odd vocal mannerism (i.e., "Myah whew!" or "D-d-d-d-doggone it, Roy!"), limping gait, bathes once a year "whether I need it or not."

ACTING STYLE: master of the double take.

PERSONALITY: stubborn, cranky, fiercely loyal to hero, character flaw (see "sugar addiction") that leads to hero's jeopardy. May have humorous musical talent. Must speak fluent gibberish, especially when riled up.

GREAT GURUS: Gabby Hayes, Fuzzy St. John, Walter Brennan.

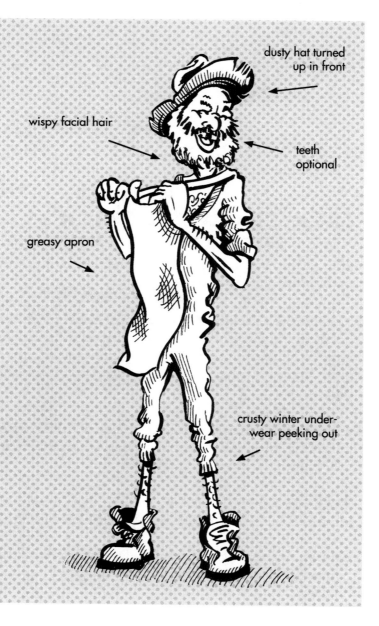

dusty hat turned up in front

wispy facial hair

teeth optional

greasy apron

crusty winter under-wear peeking out

TALK SHOW SIDEKICK

Born on the second night of earliest talk show after host realized no one knew when to laugh.

SALIENT CHARACTERISTICS: neat appearance but not quite as stylish as host, genial "everyman" persona; slightly chubby; large repertoire of appreciative laughs, from expectant grin to knowing chuckle to outright guffaw.

ACTING STYLE: wide-eyed realization of "Oh! I'm the butt of the joke!" Must be able to deliver "Great idea!" with sincerity.

PERSONALITY: agreeable, affable, may needle or tease host but must not cross invisible line to belittling.

GREAT GURUS: Ed McMahon, Durward Kirby, Paul Shaffer.

SPORTS SIDEKICK

Created when star grew tired of carrying own stuff and realized he could afford someone else to do it.

SALIENT CHARACTERISTICS: strong back, ability to turn into wallpaper when the light shines on Star. Must know Star's game but amuse star with outside interests.

GREAT GURU: Steve Williams.

SUPERHERO SIDEKICKS: A BAD IDEA

To begin with, there aren't any real superheroes, and **Robert Downey Jr.** is only a movie star with stunt doubles and access to tons of special effects. But should you one day encounter a superhero or enter an alternate universe where cities are named Gotham or Metropolis, and where people who wear blue spandex unitards, gold belts, crimson breeches, and red shoes can fly, then you could be a superhero's sidekick.

But, know this before you take it on, *it is a bad idea.* You'll often be beaten, you'll often be tortured, you'll often be mutilated, and you'll often be more or less killed (more or less because in TV soap operas and superhero world, death is never a done deal).

Does this sound like the ideal sidekick job you've been considering? No, this is the sidekick job from hell.

That's not to say this sidekick job won't have its rewards:

★ You'll most likely be rich (all superheroes have some secret source of wealth and they're good about sharing it with their sidekicks).

★ You'll have nice cars, travel the world (though generally when you travel your life will be in great danger and before your trip is over you will suffer greatly and nearly die—and not from drinking the water.

★ Occasionally you'll even have a date, but it won't be what it seems and it won't end well. And at any given moment, a power-crazed super villain may be about to strike.

No, it's not an easy gig. When it's good it goes bad and when it's bad it gets worse. It's a bad idea.

Let's take, for example, the case of Robin the "Beat Up" Boy Wonder. The most famous superhero sidekick, Robin the Boy Wonder first appeared in *Detective Comics* number 38, April 1940. His appearance brought him instant fame and glory. Hardly anyone says "Batman" without adding "and Robin."

But Robin is a case study in why being a superhero's sidekick is a bad idea. To begin with, he was given a yellow, green, and red costume—talk about being an easy target! And while he has a utility belt packed with batty tricks and can deliver a good right cross and take a punch with the best of them, he is still just a kid and no match for super villains and their over-muscled henchmen.

As a result, he has been punched, throttled and kicked from one end of Gotham City to the other. He has been mauled by manmade monsters, stabbed by mutants, shot by thugs, and even killed, more or less, by The Joker. On top of all that, he has been replaced three times: twice by other boy Robins and once by a girl! (who was murdered by the supervillain Black Mask, more or less, but still went on to be the third Batgirl.) This led to a return of Robin and this in turn . . . let's just stop now because from here on it starts to get confusing. I think you can see that Robin is no bluebird of happiness.

LIVING IN SUPERHERO CITY

Let's say the boss calls you in and tells you he's transferring you to a branch office in someplace like Gotham City, Metropolis, or Sub Diego and you suddenly find yourself in a superhero city.

Of course, this is your opportunity to sidekick up with a caped crusader. But even if better sense prevails and you run whenever you see spandex and domino masks, you'll still need to prepare for the worst. After all, a city of superheroes is also a city of supervillains.

In these cities you'll need to always be ready for extremes of weather—some ice-mad, cold-blooded villain could lower even hot summer temperatures to subzero at any given moment. Or some fiery, hot-blooded deranged villain could just as easily raise even frigid winter temperatures to equatorial extremes. Even on the balmiest of days, some inter-cosmic menace could suddenly bring an intergalactic electrical storm crashing down and unleash a firestorm of fantastic force on the city.

Then there's the sleepless villain who pumps a gas into the air that puts the entire city to sleep, or the windy villain who brings in a mega hurricane to blow the city away. The list of abuses these cities constantly endure goes on and on.

Friends, this is the stuff of daily routine in a superhero city. It's no place to live and raise a family, or even live and do anything other than prepare for the worst.

Holy Sidekick Handbook, Batman! According to this, Superhero Sidekicks like me should get extra hazard pay!

Typical daily superhero city perils

★ Deadly fogs in the morning

★ Brain worms in your Wheaties

★ Beautiful aliens who want to eat your eyes for lunch

★ Zombies at tea time

★ Giant leeches in the men's room

★ No TP in the ladies room

★ Afternoon tidal waves

★ Dinnertime earthquakes

★ Subliminal messages from your tv that make you buy things you don't want, okay that could happen anywhere.

★ Multi-tentacled creatures slithering out from under your bed during the night

★ Nightmares and you're not sleeping

★ And that's only on weekdays, weekends are worse.

SUPERHERO SIDEKICK

Typically a pint-sized version of the superhero. Came to prominence in the 1940s to give kids a character to relate to in superhero adventures.

OUTFITS: must be color-coordinated with the superhero, and feature a younger, smaller version of the superhero's icon. For example, if the superhero sports a blazing sun, the sidekick might have a lightbulb. If the superhero is known by his Bengal tiger patch, the sidekick would wear a stylized tabby cat.

TRAITS: brave, ready for thrills, eager to throw self into harm's way, just headstrong enough to get in over his head and need the superhero to bail him out. Once in awhile, however, proves worth by bailing out the superhero. Fabulous hair a plus.

KING OF SUPERHERO SIDEKICKS: Robin. Made his trademark dialogue ("Holy Sidekick Vocal Shtick, Batman!") into a short-lived national craze.

eager expression

stance that
says,
"I can take
'em on!"

younger, smaller
version of super-
hero's icon

outfit coordinates
with superhero's

J.J.'S THREE KEYS TO BEING A POLITICIAN'S SIDEKICK

J.J. "Let's Call Him Smith" is a longtime politician's sidekick we met who refuses to go on the record, name names, or reveal details about anyone or anything he knows. In addition to having been appointed to innumerable better government committees, J.J. also serves on the board of several Washington think tanks, even though he's never spent a lot of time thinking. He's a frequent guest at White House dinners and has traveled first class all over the world on numerous political junkets. These are J.J.'s three keys to being a politician's sidekick:

First off, pick a politician you actually like. They already have to put up with enough people who see them walking down the street and say, "There goes Senator Horse's Ass." They sure won't put up with a sidekick who says it too.

Second, stay on the sunny side of the aisle and keep away from shady back room deals—that's a place for Turd Blossoms and Serpentheads. Sidekicks don't cross the line. Their role is to keep it on the road and provide friendship and laughs along the way.

Third, remember birthdays and anniversaries but forget golf scores.

Fourth, stay out of the limelight and off television talk shows. The less exposure you have to the outside world, the more you can be a trusted not to spill the beans.

Fifth, never write a book.

Sixth, never leak information, never be a source, never come in through the front door.

Seventh, and most important, vote for your politician and encourage others to do the same.

POLITICAL SIDEKICK

Not a political operative, more a salve for the candidate's perpetually bruised ego. Must be conversant with some degree of political nuance, but never a threat to take over the campaign. Access to a great deal of money is a plus. A great guy to have a beer with and blow off a little steam. Can tell an ethnic joke flawlessly. He'd never write a tell-all book because "heck, we're talkin' about my friend here!"

James Carville's stellar sidekick work (funny bald head, funny accent) with Bill Clinton continued the great tradition of presidential sidekicks, stretching back to FDR's Louis Howe with his wrinkled suit sprinkled with cigarette ashes, Truman's poker buddies, and Nixon's confidant and last defender, banker Bebe Rebozo.

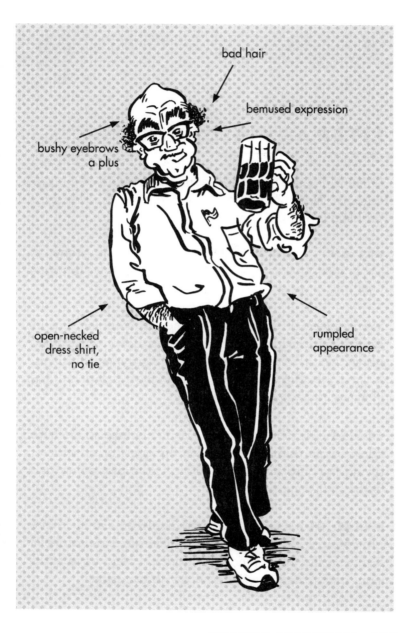

LITERARY SIDEKICK

Often a chubbier, less well-educated version of the protagonist. May provide a skill or be able to solve some problem along the way.

SALIENT CHARACTERISTICS: Possibly prone to sage, folksy wisdom, e.g., "Ain't but two ways to argue with a woman, and they're both wrong."

Weaknesses or flaws point up hero's strengths. For instance, a sidekick who clumsily falls down while tying his shoelace adds import to the hero's gymnastic stunts. A drunken sidekick emphasizes the hero's clear-headed thinking. Adds ironic counterpoint.

TRAITS: Must be a little slow on the uptake so the hero can explain again why he's on his quest or adventure, giving the hero an opportunity to relate plot points and flesh out his character.

GREAT GURUS: Falstaff and Samwise Gamgee are prototypical, but Sancho Panza, illiterate-and-proud-of-it squire, is the gold standard. "I drink when I have occasion, and sometimes when I have no occasion."

rosy cheeks that speak of fresh country air or too much drink

chubby, less well-educated appearance

pipe for smoking while dispensing country wisdom

IN CONCLUSION: THE SIDEKICK FLU

Yes, the sidekick life is a great life, and now that we've shown you the way, inner peace and happiness are yours. And sure, your own life and satisfaction are big deals, but get a few million miles under your tires like we have and you'll come to realize that it's not just about you. There's the world and all creation to think about. How does the sidekick fit in? And we mean cosmically.

It might be helpful to imagine a Sidekick Flu, a fast-moving infection that burns through the culture, killing off only the sidekicks. It's a grim scenario, but once we've eulogized them with a "Yes, they were odd, but they made us laugh," carted their Hawaiian-shirted corpses to the graveyard, said a tearful goodbye, and shoveled in the dirt, what are we left with?

We'll tell you what: a meal with a meaty entree, but no sides, no spice, no drink, and no dessert—that's what.

We're left with Don Quixote de la Mancha toting his own armor, adrift in insanity with no Sancho Panza to play the role of us, the eyes and voices of tolerant good humor and reason. Not much of a book.

We're left with Prince Hal and about a quarter of a play, with no Falstaff chewing the scenery, no bawdy counterpoint to the reconciliation of the Prince with his destiny, no recognition of our shared earthy humanity. Not much of a play.

We're left reading about Sherlock Holmes operating as a lone wolf, difficult and unknowable, without Dr. Watson to let us know that Holmes must be a good guy, because Watson likes him. Not much of a story.

We're left watching Harry Potter make his solitary way through Hogwarts, befriended certainly by Hermione and Neville, but missing goofy Ron Weasley and his oafish jokes and camaraderie. Without a pal, it's not much of a coming-of-age.

Not to put too fine a point on it, but in short, without side-kicks we're left with . . . not much. Just a drab, fearfully serious and self-important world that no one would care to live in.

So next time you swoon over a hero, next time your pulse races with plot-driven fever, next time you laugh at a left-field turn of phrase, remember to take a moment and thank the sidekick that made it possible. And what the heck, buy him lunch.

Friend, as a newly minted sidekick you work in a long and noble tradition. Go forth, prosper, sow your sidekick seeds, and remember, always in life, "Myah Whew!"

ABOUT THE

AUTHORS

TOO SLIM, whippet-thin bespectacled bassist and comedian for Western Music's masters of outdoor harmony and multiple Grammy winners Riders In The Sky, is the only cowboy sidekick currently making a living.

He is the only known songwriter to have songs recorded by Tammy Wynette, William Shatner, and Don Rickles, a feat he describes as the "mythical trifecta."

Writing under the name of wiseacre Fred LaBour, Too Slim was responsible for the satirical fake news story that gave life to the "Paul McCartney Is Dead" rumor many years ago. You can look it up.

He is well known in small circles for numerous mic bits, zany take-offs, japes and put-ons of the highest and lowest order, as well as poetry, which his beautiful wife Roberta often reviews as something that "ought to be in a book."

He lives on the Too Ranch near Nashville with his inspiring family, raising children, ticks and slugs.

Too Slim and Texas Bix Bender have collaborated for nearly three decades, devising hundreds of scripts for public radio's *Riders Radio Theatre*, the late-night cowboy movie show *Tumbleweed Theatre*, and various stage and TV specials.

TEXAS BIX BENDER has become one of America's best-known Western humorists and philosophers. He is the author of eighteen books, including the best-selling *Don't Squat With Yer Spurs On: A Cowboy's Guide To Life*.

Prior to this he worked as a writer for *Hee Haw* and as a writer/producer for The Nashville Network, where he produced *Tumbleweed Theater: Starring Riders In The Sky*. In 1989, he began to co-write and appear on the public radio program *Riders Radio Theatre*.

The humor and wisdom of Texas Bix Bender have been quoted by Jack Welch, former chairman of General Electric, radio legend Paul Harvey, Click and Clack on their National Public Radio program *Car Talk*, cowboys all over the West, and thousands of bartenders from coast to coast. His books have been read on *Oprah*, quoted in the pages of *Forbes*, and quoted by generals in the Pentagon.

Despite all this, he remains a simple millionaire half-assed cowboy and resides on a small salsa spread on the outskirts of Nashville, where he runs a herd of jalapeños, habañeros, and cayennes with a few beefsteak tomatoes and an undisciplined plot of cilantro.

SIDE MEAT, consultant to the authors and expert on all things sidekick, has been camp cook for America's Favorite Cowboys, Riders In The Sky, for more than thirty years.

His culinary "expertise," trademark wheeze "Myah whew!" and unerring comedic interruptions have catapulted him to the forefront of the thin, nearly depopulated ranks of cowboy sidekicks.

Mr. Meat, of indeterminate age and lineage (although he refers to one "Mama Meat" on holidays), has prospected for gold and cooked his way "around the world and then some—myah whew!"

He apparently was present at the Alaskan Gold Rush of '97, where "I found the Mother Lode. I swear I found it." After a riotous celebration in Skagway, an inebriated Mr. Meat fell into a glacial crevasse, was flash frozen and remained in cryogenic suspended animation for 80 years. "Like Tombstone, he was too tough to die," said one doctor present at Side Meat's thawing out after the crusty coot was discovered by a highway crew blasting a road cut in 1980.

He then signed on with Riders In The Sky to save the show and cook plenty of his beans and biscuits, which are known throughout the West as "The Hardest Substance Known to Man."

Side Meat can currently be heard interrupting and gumming up the works on Sirius/XM radio's *Ranger Doug's Classic Cowboy Corral.*